High–Frequency Sight Words
Literacy Skills Series

• • • • • • • • • • • • • • • • •

Written by Staci Marck

GRADE K-1

Classroom Complete Press
P.O. Box 19729
San Diego, CA 92159
Tel: 1-800-663-3609 | Fax: 1-800-663-3608
Email: service@classroomcompletepress.com

www.classroomcompletepress.com

ISBN-13: 978-1-55319-405-7
ISBN-10: 1-55319-405-5
© 2009

Permission to Reproduce

Permission is granted to the individual teacher who purchases one copy of this book to reproduce the student activity material for use in his or her classroom only. Reproduction of these materials for colleagues, an entire school or school system, or for commercial sale is strictly prohibited. No part of this publication may be transmitted in any form or by any means, electronic, mechanical, recording or otherwise without the prior written permission of the publisher. We acknowledge the financial support of the Government of Canada through the Book Publishing Industry Development Program (BPIDP) for our publishing activities. Printed in Canada. All rights reserved.

Critical Thinking Skills

High-Frequency Sight Words Grade K-1

Skills For Critical Thinking		Boxed Words	Mixed Up Words	Sentence Completion	Match and Print	Sight Word Stories	Writing Tasks	Crossword	Word Search	Graphic Organizers
LEVEL 1 Remembering	• Identify	✓		✓	✓	✓		✓	✓	✓
	• Read	✓	✓	✓	✓	✓	✓	✓	✓	✓
	• Match	✓	✓	✓	✓	✓				
	• Select	✓	✓	✓	✓	✓				✓
	• Record	✓	✓	✓	✓	✓				✓
LEVEL 2 Understanding	• Use				✓		✓			✓
	• Describe									✓
	• Reorganize		✓							
	• Interpret			✓					✓	✓
LEVEL 3 Applying	• Choose Information			✓	✓		✓		✓	✓
	• Construct									✓
	• Apply What Is Learned	✓	✓	✓			✓		✓	✓
LEVEL 4 Analysing	• Discriminate	✓	✓	✓	✓	✓	✓	✓	✓	✓
	• Illustrate				✓		✓			✓
	• Identify Relationships					✓		✓		✓
LEVEL 5 Evaluating	• Decide						✓	✓		✓
	• Make Choices			✓	✓	✓	✓			✓
	• Explain						✓			
LEVEL 6 Creating	• Design (i.e., a picture book)						✓			✓
	• Create						✓			✓

Based on Bloom's Taxonomy

Contents

🍎 TEACHER GUIDE
- Critical Thinking Skills 2
- Assessment Rubric 4
- Teacher Guide 5
- Graphic Organizers 6
- Bloom's Taxonomy & Vocabulary 7

✏️ STUDENT WORKSHEETS
- Boxed Words 9
- Mixed Up Words 22
- Sentence Completion 28
- Match and Print 31
- Sight Word Stories 34
- Writing Tasks 37
- Sight Word Flash Cards 40
- Crossword 46
- Word Search 47
- Comprehension Quiz 48

EZ✓ EASY MARKING™ ANSWER KEY 50

GRAPHIC ORGANIZERS 55

✔ **6 BONUS Activity Pages!** Additional worksheets for your students **FREE!**

- Go to our website: **www.classroomcompletepress.com/bonus**
- Enter item CC1113 or High-Frequency Sight Words
- Enter pass code CC1113D for Activity Pages

Assessment Rubric

High-Frequency Sight Words Grade K-1

Student's Name: _____ Assignment: _____ Level: _____

	Level 1	Level 2	Level 3	Level 4
Sight Word Recognition	• Recognizes a few sight words	• Recognizes some sight words	• Recognizes most sight words	• Recognizes all sight words
Rhyme Awareness	• Recognizes when a few words rhyme	• Recognizes when some words rhyme	• Recognizes when most words rhyme	• Recognizes when all words rhyme
Identifies Beginning Sounds/Letters in Words	• Identifies a few beginning sounds/letters of sight words (g – good)	• Identifies some beginning sounds/letters of sight words (g – good)	• Identifies most beginning sounds/letters of sight words (g – good)	• Thoroughly identifies beginning sounds/letters of sight words (g – good)
Use the Shape of the Word to Identify it and Write it	• Uses a few letter shapes to identify and write words	• Uses some letter shapes to identify and write words	• Uses many letter shapes to identify and write words	• Always uses shapes to identify and write words
Sentence Creation	• Creates a few simple sentences that are slightly clear	• Creates some simple sentences that are moderately clear	• Creates many sentences that are usually clear	• Creates sentences that are extremely clear

STRENGTHS:

WEAKNESSES:

NEXT STEPS:

Before You Teach

Teacher Guide

Our resource has been created for ease of use by both TEACHERS and STUDENTS alike.

Introduction

Increase sight word recognition, vocabulary and comprehension as you help your students identify sight words using real life pictures as an aid. Sight words are words that must become automatically recognized by the reader because they are often not pronounced or spelled in regular ways; and because approximately 100 high-frequency words make up at least 50 percent of everything that we read as adults. As students begin to read and build their sight word knowledge, they will build a bank of known vocabulary words that will aid them in beginning to read and spell. Boxes are used to help students come to understand that words can be recognized by the shapes of their letters, as they contain small, tall or hanging letters. Reproducible work sheets include mixed up words, boxed words, writing, cloze sentences, stories and puzzles. This resource provides ready-to-use information and activities for beginning readers. It can be used in any Language Arts program as a supplement to a balanced literacy program to strengthen children's reading, writing and thinking skills.

Words are best learned in context. It is best to introduce the activities in this book as they appear in your Shared Reading, Guided Reading, Writing and Words blocks. Highlight them as they are encountered in print sources every day. As the words are introduced, place them on your Word Wall to help students learn letters and words and become more independent readers and writers. Generally five words are introduced in a five-day week. The words are practiced and reinforced all week and placed on the Word Wall on Friday.

How Is Our Resource Organized?

Activities in language, reading comprehension and writing (in the form of reproducible worksheets) make up the majority of our resource. There are a variety of pages organized in the following sections: BOXED WORDS activities, MIXED UP WORDS activities, CLOZE activities, MATCH AND PRINT activities, SIGHT WORD STORY activities, and WRITING tasks. All are either a half-page or full page long.

It is not expected that all activities will be used, but are provided for variety and flexibility in the resource.

- Flash cards are provided to help build student recognition of words. Reproduce them, cut them apart and mount them on a sturdy back and laminate. Make several sets in order to make games like "Concentration" and "Go Fish". Copies of flash cards could also be sent home to build student knowledge and understanding of picture words.

- Also provided are two puzzles, a word search and crossword. Each of these worksheets can be completed as individual activities or done in pairs.

- Six Graphic Organizers are included to help develop students' thinking and writing skills. The Assessment Rubric (page 4) is a useful tool for evaluating students' responses to many of the activities in our resource. The Comprehension Quiz (page 48) can be used for either a follow-up review or assessment at the completion of the unit.

EASY MARKING™ ANSWER KEY

Marking students' worksheets is fast and easy with our **Answer Key**. Answers are listed in columns – just line up the column with its corresponding worksheet, as shown, and see how every question matches up with its answer!

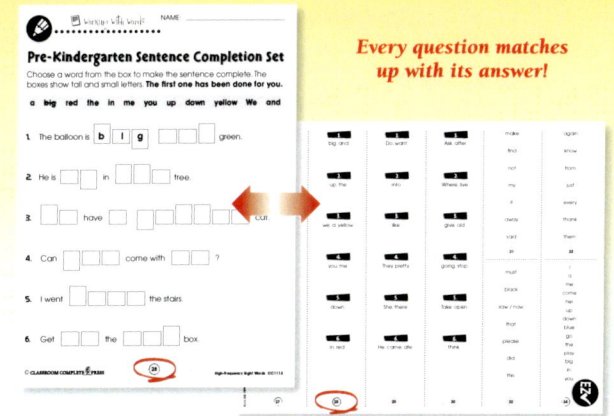

Every question matches up with its answer!

Before You Teach

1, 2, 3, 4, 5, 6 Graphic Organizers

Suggestions for using the six **Graphic Organizers** included in our **Sight Word Book** are found below. They may also be adapted to suit the individual needs of your students. The organizers can be used on a projection system or interactive whiteboard in teacher-led activities, and/or photocopied for use as student worksheets. To evaluate students' responses to any of the organizers, you may wish to use the **Assessment Rubric** (on page 4). Once each activity has been taught and practiced many times, it can become a center or be used as an individual activity.

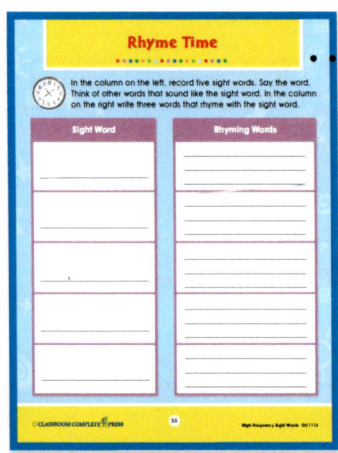

RHYME TIME

This organizer can be used as a whole class activity and then as a small group or individual activity. To introduce this to the whole class, talk about rhyming words. Ask students: How do you know when words rhyme? Do these words rhyme – boy/girl, ate/date, at/cat, big/large? When you are confident that the majority of the students understand rhyming words, ask students to suggest sight words that they know. Create a list on the board of all the suggestions. Choose five words from the list that you can find rhyming words for. One at a time orally manipulate each word to create real and nonsense words. Ask students to listen to each rhyming word: Does the word make sense? Does it sound right? Together determine if it is a real word. Record three real rhyming words for each sight word, then do the same process for the next sight word until the sheet is complete. **Found on Page 55.**

WRITE THE ROOM

This organizer can be used as a whole class, small group or individual activity. Ask students to look around the classroom for sight words. Together brainstorm a list of sight words found in the classroom. Choose ten words. Write one on each line. Write a sentence using five of the words. At first, the group may need manipulatives to assist them with this activity. You could provide students with the flash cards to help them identify sight words. **Found on Page 56.**

TAKE A GUESS

This organizer can be used as a whole class, small group or individual activity. For a class activity, lead your students through how to successfully complete this activity. Prior to beginning the activity, pick a sight word. Fill in the clues. Together brainstorm 3-4 possible answers to each clue in the side margin. Model how to eliminate guesses that do not fit the subsequent clues.

Extend the activity by having students write their own sentence using the word. **Found on Page 57.**

Before You Teach

1, 2, 3, 4, 5, 6
Graphic Organizers

SIGHT WORD TALLY CHART

This organizer can be used as a whole class, small group or individual activity. For a whole class activity, use a shared reading text that students are familiar with. Read one page at a time and together identify sight words. Read up to five pages until ten sight words are found. Place a tally in the column on the right every time the word appears in the text. Once the sheet has been completed, review the sight words and tallies. Which word appeared most often in the text? Which words appeared the same number of times? **Found on Page 58.**

PREDICT THE HIDDEN WORD

This organizer is a whole class and/or small group activity. Place a sticky note on the pictures in the story. Read the title to the students and ask them about the park and what kind of things happen there. Ask students to predict which word is hidden as you read the passage aloud. In the side margin record three student predictions for each word covered. Reveal one letter at a time for the covered words. As each letter is revealed:
- Ask the students if the predictions look possible. (Does the first letter match each predicted word?)
- Ask the students if they would like to cross any out.
- Would they like to change their predictions. Why or why not?
- Adjust words accordingly.
- Circle the word that matches the prediction as letters are revealed.
- Revealing the picture, does the word match the picture?

Celebrate all of the words that the students accurately predict. **Found on Page 59.**

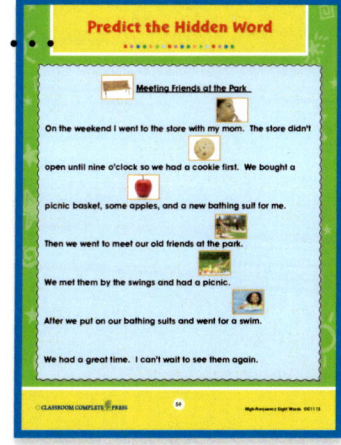

ENDINGS

This organizer can be used as a whole class, small group or individual activity. For a whole class or small group activity, model adding word endings to sight words to form new words before asking students to try the activity on their own. As whole group, model the procedure using the organizer several times until students are proficient.
- Write the word: *looks*.
- He *looks* great in his new shirt.
- Which sight word will help you spell *looks*? (look)
- What ending do we need to add to *look* to spell *looks*? (-s)
- *looks*

Found on Page 60.

Bloom's Taxonomy* for Reading Comprehension

The activities in this resource engage and build the full range of thinking skills that are essential for students' reading comprehension. Based on the six levels of thinking in Bloom's Taxonomy, questions are given that challenge students to not only recall what they have read, but to move beyond this to understand the text through higher-order thinking. By using higher-order skills of applying, analysing, evaluating and creating, students become active readers, drawing more meaning from the text, and applying and extending their learning in more sophisticated ways.

Our **High-Frequency Sight Words Book**, therefore, is an effective tool for any Language Arts program. Whether it is used in whole or in part, or adapted to meet individual student needs, this resource provides teachers with the important questions to ask, inspiring students' interest, creativity, and promoting meaningful learning.

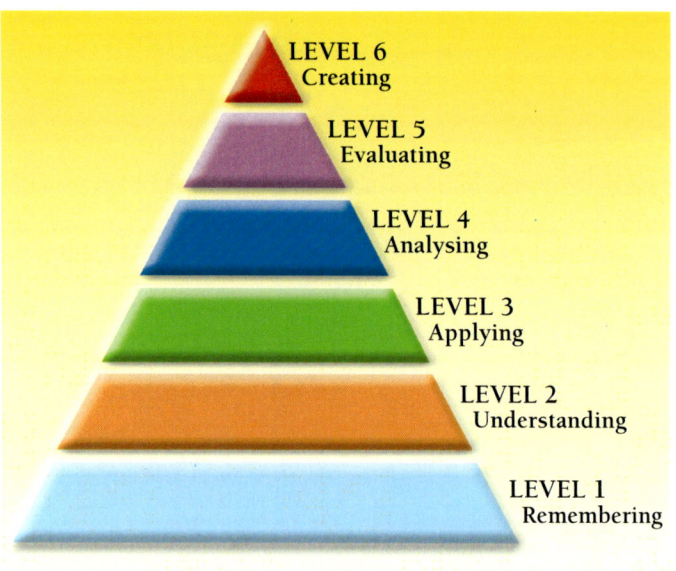

**BLOOM'S TAXONOMY:
6 LEVELS OF THINKING**

Bloom's Taxonomy is a tool widely used by educators for classifying learning objectives, and is based on the work of Benjamin Bloom.

Dolch Sight Words

Pre-Kindergarten

a	jump	we
and	little	yellow
away	look	you
big	make	
blue	me	
can	my	
come	not	
down	one	
find	play	
for	red	
funny	run	
go	said	
help	see	
hers	the	
I	three	
in	to	
is	two	
it	up	

Kindergarten

all	into	that
am	like	there
are	must	they
at	new	this
ate	no	too
be	now	under
black	on	want
brown	our	was
but	out	well
came	please	went
did	pretty	what
do	ran	white
eat	ride	who
four	saw	will
get	say	with
good	she	yes
has	so	
he	soon	

Grade 1

after	just	think
again	know	walk
an	let	where
any	live	when
as	may	
ask	of	
by	old	
could	once	
every	open	
fly	over	
from	put	
give	round	
going	some	
had	stop	
has	take	
her	thank	
him	them	
how	then	

NAME: _____

Pre-Kindergarten Boxed Words Set #1

Use each word in the list once. Write the letters in the boxes that match the shape of the word. The boxes show tall and small letters.

a   big   red   the   in   me   you   up   down   go

1. ☐☐   6. ☐☐☐
2. ☐   7. ☐☐☐☐
3. ☐☐   8. ☐☐
4. ☐☐☐   9. ☐☐☐
5. ☐☐   10. ☐☐☐

Write a sentence using one of the sight words.
_____
_____

© CLASSROOM COMPLETE PRESS   9   High-Frequency Sight Words CC1113

NAME: _____

Pre-Kindergarten Boxed Words Set#2

Use each word in the list once. Write the letters in the boxes that match the shape of the word. The boxes show tall and small letters.

I   can   jump   we   run   to   is   for   help   not

1.
2.
3.
4.
5.
6.
7.
8.
9.
10.

Write a sentence using one of the sight words.

_____
_____

NAME: _____

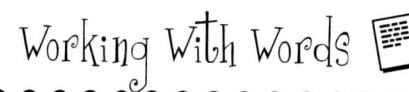 

Pre-Kindergarten Boxed Words Set #3

Use each word in the list once. Write the letters in the boxes that match the shape of the word. The boxes show tall and small letters.

and   blue   come   find   her   it   little   my   play   said

1.
2.
3.
4.
5.
6.
7.
8.
9.
10.

Write a sentence using one of the sight words.
_____
_____

Pre-Kindergarten Boxed Words Set #4

Use each word in the list once. Write the letters in the boxes that match the shape of the word. The boxes show tall and small letters.

away   funny   look   make   one   see   three   two   yellow

1.
2.
3.
4.
5.
6.
7.
8.
9.

Write a sentence using one of the sight words.

_____
_____

NAME: _____

Kindergarten Boxed Words Set #1

Use each word in the list once. Write the letters in the boxes that match the shape of the word. The boxes show tall and small letters.

all   did   good   must   our   ride   soon   too   went   with

1. ☐☐☐☐
2. ☐☐☐☐
3. ☐☐☐☐
4. ☐☐☐☐
5. ☐☐☐

6. ☐☐☐☐
7. ☐☐☐☐
8. ☐☐☐
9. ☐☐☐
10. ☐☐☐

Write two sentences using one sight word in each one.

_____
_____

Kindergarten Boxed Words Set#2

Use each word in the list once. Write the letters in the boxes that match the shape of the word. The boxes show tall and small letters.

am   black   do   new   out   saw   that   under   what   yes

1.
2.
3.
4.
5.
6.
7.
8.
9.
10.

Write two sentences using one sight word in each one.

_____
_____

NAME: _____

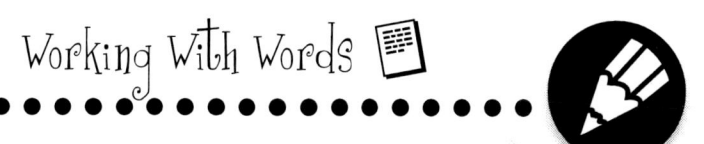

Kindergarten Boxed Words Set #3

Use each word in the list once. Write the letters in the boxes that match the shape of the word. The boxes show tall and small letters.

are   brown   eat   he   no   please   say   there   want   white

1. ☐☐☐
2. ☐☐☐☐☐
3. ☐☐☐☐☐
4. ☐☐☐☐
5. ☐☐☐
6. ☐☐
7. ☐☐
8. ☐☐☐☐☐
9. ☐☐☐☐
10. ☐☐☐

Write two sentences using one sight word in each one.

_____
_____

NAME: _____

Kindergarten Boxed Words Set #4

Use each word in the list once. Write the letters in the boxes that match the shape of the word. The boxes show tall and small letters.

| at | but | four | into | now | pretty | she | they | was | who |

1. ☐☐☐☐
2. ☐☐☐☐
3. ☐☐
4. ☐☐☐☐
5. ☐☐☐
6. ☐☐
7. ☐☐☐
8. ☐☐☐☐☐☐
9. ☐☐☐
10. ☐☐☐

Write two sentences using one sight word in each one.

_____
_____

NAME: _____

Kindergarten Boxed Words Set#5

Use each word in the list once. Write the letters in the boxes that match the shape of the word. The boxes show tall and small letters.

ate   came   get   like   on   ran   so   this   well   will

1.
2.
3.
4.
5.
6.
7.
8.
9.
10.

Write two sentences using one sight word in each one.

_____
_____

First Grade Boxed Words #1

Use each word in the list once. Write the letters in the boxes that match the shape of the word. The boxes show tall and small letters.

after   as   every   going   him   let   old   put   take   think

1. ☐☐☐
2. ☐☐☐☐☐
3. ☐☐☐
4. ☐☐
5. ☐☐☐

6. ☐☐
7. ☐☐☐
8. ☐☐☐☐
9. ☐☐☐☐
10. ☐☐☐☐

Write two sentences using one sight word in each one.

_____

_____

NAME: _____

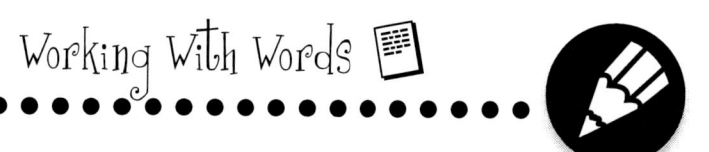

First Grade Boxed Words #2

Use each word in the list once. Write the letters in the boxes that match the shape of the word. The boxes show tall and small letters.

again   ask   fly   had   how   live   once   round   thank   walk

1.
2.
3.
4.
5.
6.
7.
8.
9.
10.

Write two sentences using one sight word in each one.
_____
_____

First Grade Boxed Words #3

Use each word in the list once. Write the letters in the boxes that match the shape of the word. The boxes show tall and small letters.

an   by   from   has   just   may   open   some   them   where

1.
2.
3.
4.
5.
6.
7.
8.
9.
10.

Write two sentences using one sight word in each one.

NAME: _____

First Grade Boxed Words #4

Use each word in the list once. Write the letters in the boxes that match the shape of the word. The boxes show tall and small letters.

any   could   give   her   know   of   over   stop   then   when

1. ☐☐☐
2. ☐☐☐☐
3. ☐☐☐☐
4. ☐☐☐☐
5. ☐☐☐
6. ☐☐☐☐
7. ☐☐
8. ☐☐☐☐
9. ☐☐☐☐
10. ☐☐☐

Write two sentences using one sight word in each one.

_____
_____

© CLASSROOM COMPLETE PRESS

21

High-Frequency Sight Words CC1113

Pre-Kindergarten Mixed Up Words Set #1

Unscramble the sight words. **Write the word on the lines.**

nwod

_____

mjpu

_____

otw

_____

kolo

_____

nfyun

_____

nru

_____

NAME: _____

Working With Words

Pre-Kindergarten Mixed Up Words Set #2

Unscramble the words. **Write the word on the lines.**

gbi

_____

anc

_____

eon

_____

plhe

_____

eehrt

_____

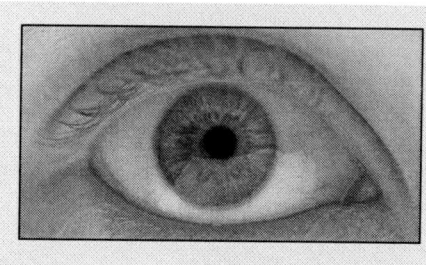

ese

_____

Kindergarten Mixed Up Words Set#1

Unscramble the sight words. **Write the word on the lines.**

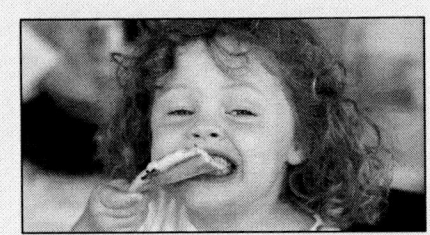
aet

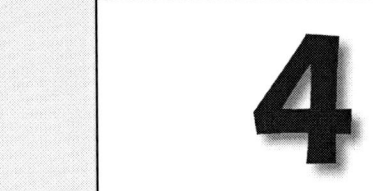
uofr

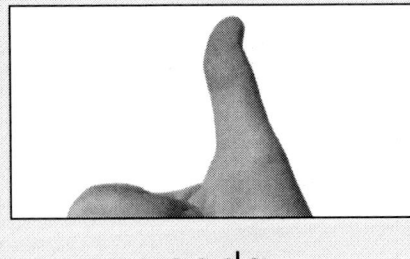
oodg

ewn

on

uot

NAME: _____

Working With Words

Kindergarten Mixed Up Words Set#2

Unscramble the words. **Write the word on the lines.**

anr

_____

edir

_____

dnuer

_____

llwe

_____

sye

_____

rtteyp

_____

Grade One Mixed Up Words Set #1

Unscramble the sight words. **Write the word on the lines.**

kas

yfl

erh family

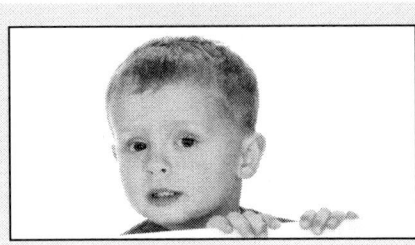

mhi

vgie

dol

Working With Words

Grade One Mixed Up Words Set#2

Unscramble the words. **Write the word on the lines.**

epno

_____

eovr

_____

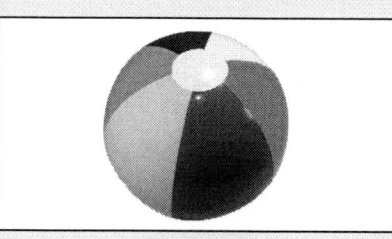

urdon

_____

opts

_____

hktni

_____

kawl

_____

Pre-Kindergarten Sentence Completion Set

Choose a word from the box to make the sentence complete. The boxes show tall and small letters. **The first one has been done for you.**

a ~~big~~ red the in me you up down yellow We and

1. The balloon is **b i g** ☐☐☐ green.

2. He is ☐☐ in ☐☐☐ tree.

3. ☐☐ have ☐ ☐☐☐☐☐ cat.

4. Can ☐☐☐ come with ☐☐ ?

5. I went ☐☐☐☐ the stairs.

6. Get ☐☐ the ☐☐☐ box.

Kindergarten Sentence Completion Set

Choose a word from the box to make the sentence complete. The boxes show tall and small letters. **The first one has been done for you.**

He   like   pretty   She   there   They   ate   came   into   ~~Do~~   want

1. **D** **o** you ☐☐☐☐ to come to my house?

2. I am going to jump ☐☐☐☐ the pool.

3. Would you ☐☐☐☐ a piece of cake?

4. ☐☐☐☐ live in a ☐☐☐☐☐☐ house.

5. ☐☐☐ is over ☐☐☐☐☐ by the tree.

6. ☐☐ ☐☐☐☐ over to my house and ☐☐☐ .

First Grade Sentence Completion Set

Choose a word from the box to make the sentence complete. The boxes show tall and small letters. **The first one has been done for you.**

~~Ask~~   open   give   going   old   think   Where   Take   stop   live   after

1. **A s k** your mom if you can play ☐☐☐☐ school.

2. ☐☐☐☐ do you ☐☐☐☐ ?

3. Could you ☐☐☐☐ me your ☐☐☐ bike to ride?

4. We are ☐☐☐☐☐ to ☐☐☐☐ at the park on the way home.

5. ☐☐☐ my keys and ☐☐☐☐ the door.

6. What do you ☐☐☐☐ the answer is?

NAME: _____

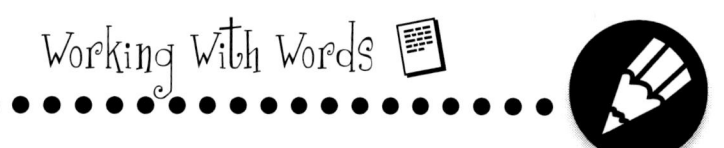

Pre-Kindergarten Match and Print Words Set

Examine the word box. Select the words that match the shape of the word. Write a letter from the word in each box until the boxes are all filled. Then print the word on the lines.

| away | find | for | is | it | make | my | not | said | to |

# Kindergarten Match and Print Words Set

Examine the word box. Select the words that match the shape of the word. Write a letter from the word in each box until the boxes are all filled. Then print the word on the lines.

all   black   did   has   must   now   please   saw   that   this

NAME: _____

Working With Words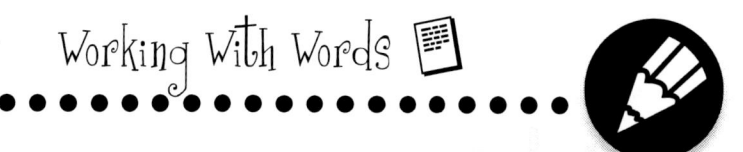

Grade One Match and Print Words Set

Examine the word box. Select the words that match the shape of the word. Write a letter from the word in each box until the boxes are all filled. Then print the word on the lines.

| as | again | any | every | from | had | just | know | thank | them |

Pre-Kindergarten Sight Word Story

Complete the paragraph. Use the words in the word box. Cross off each word after you use it.

a   play   big   blue   the   in   me   you   up   down
I   go   come   her

My Pet Cat

___ have ___ . She likes to kiss ___ ___ on

the 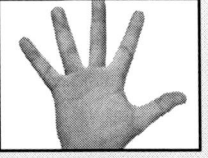. She will ___ ___ ___ ___ when I call

___ ___ ___. She jumps ___ ___ and ___ ___ ___ ___.

She has a ___ ___ ___ ___ . We like to

___ ___ to ___ ___ park.

She likes to ___ ___ ___ ___ with the ___ ___ ___

 ___ ___ the .

Do ___ ___ ___ have a pet?

NAME: _____

Kindergarten Sight Word Story

Complete the paragraph. Use the words in the word box. Cross off each word after you use it.

all   with   good   please   want   ride   soon   too   went   with

Can we go to the Park?

Can we ___ ___ ___ go to the [ferris wheel] to play? I want to go on the big [roller coaster] ___ ___ ___ ___. Do you want to go on the [slide] ___ ___ ___ ___ me? How ___ ___ ___ ___ can we go? If I am ___ ___ ___ ___, can I get a [ice cream] ___ ___ ___ ___ ___ ___ ? My friend ___ ___ ___ ___ to the [ferris wheel] ___ ___ ___ ___ her. I ___ ___ ___ to go ___ ___ ___ ___. Can we?

Working With Words

NAME: _____

Grade One Sight Word Story

Complete the paragraph. Use the words in the word box. Cross off each word after you use it.

> over   could   take   walk   by   old   After   where   open   fly   Ask

Come Over to My House

Can you come ___ ___ ___ ___ to my _____ ?

We ___ ___ ___ ___ ___ go for a ___ ___ ___ ___ to the _____. We can ___ ___ ___ my _____

___ ___ ___ ___ ___ ___ ___ the ___ ___ ___ ___ _____ is.

___ ___ ___ ___ ___ we can ___ ___ ___ ___ my _____

_____ for a run ___ ___ my ___ ___ ___ _____.

___ ___ ___ your mom if you can come.

Finish the Story

A story beginning has been given to you. Draw a picture and finish writing the story. Make sure you use at least six of your sight words.

Sight Words: _____ _____ _____
_____ _____ _____

One sunny morning I was walking along when suddenly….

_____
_____
_____
_____
_____
_____
_____
_____

 Writing Task #2

Rebus Story

A rebus story uses pictures to help the reader read the hard words in the story. Create a story using pictures and at least six of your sight words.

For example: I like to eat

Sight Words: _____ _____ _____
_____ _____ _____

Writing Task #3

Story Train

Write and illustrate a short story. Tell what happens in the beginning, in the middle and at the end. Make sure you spell your sight words correctly!

Beginning:

Middle:

End:

NAME: _____

Pre-Kindergarten Flash Cards

a	and	away
big	blue	can
come	down	find
for	funny	go
help	her	I
in	is	it
jump	little	look

NAME: _____

Flash Cards

make	me	my
not	one	play
red	run	said
see	the	three
to	two	up
we	yellow	you

Kindergarten Flash Cards

| | | all |
| am | are | at |

Flash Cards

NAME: _____

ate	be	black
brown	but	came
did	do	eat
four	get	good
has	he	into
like	must	new
no	now	on
our	out	please

NAME: _____

Flash Cards

pretty	ran	ride
saw	say	she
so	soon	that
there	they	this
too	under	want
was	well	went
what	white	who
will	with	yes

43

High-Frequency Sight Words CC1113

NAME: _____

Grade One Flash Cards

after	again	an
any	as	ask
by	could	every
fly	from	give
going	had	has
her	him	how
just	know	let

NAME: _____

Flash Cards

live	may	of
old	once	open
over	put	round
some	stop	take
thank	them	then
think	walk	where
when		

Crossword Puzzle

Word List
down, little, too, when
eat, our, two, white
every, once, under, yellow
find, red, want
four, round, we
know, thank, who

Across
1. when you are hungry, you…
3. to discover
5. it belongs to us - _____ house
6. one time
7. all is this shape
9. the sun is this color
11. ___? What? Where? When? Why?
12. my cheeks turn this color when I am angry or upset
13. use your manners: please and _____ you
14. you and I
16. small

Down
1. all
2. also
3. one, two, three, …
4. opposite of "up"
8. below the ground
10. the opposite of black is…
11. at what time
14. to have need of
15. to understand
17. one plus one

MY NAME: _____

 Hands-On Activities

Word Search

Find all of the words in the Word Search. Words are written horizontally, vertically, diagonally, and some are even written backwards.

Pre-K
and	it
blue	jump
down	make
funny	play
help	said

K
are	like
but	our
came	please
eat	there
good	what

Gr. 1
again	know
could	live
every	old
from	some
going	think

r	d	s	r	o	h	f	r	a	g	a	i	n	t	o	b
a	n	p	d	o	w	n	d	n	n	s	q	a	s	u	t
c	a	r	e	h	h	r	a	d	i	s	r	a	t	t	w
a	p	p	v	e	a	e	d	u	o	l	d	i	h	r	c
k	e	b	e	a	t	f	m	m	g	e	o	l	i	v	e
n	n	l	r	t	d	t	a	d	l	e	s	s	n	q	m
o	c	a	y	y	i	e	u	l	b	p	o	f	k	a	a
w	i	a	w	n	d	a	f	o	a	t	h	r	r	d	c
o	l	o	c	k	n	t	a	u	l	g	o	o	d	t	i
p	a	t	w	h	n	u	z	c	p	l	m	m	b	y	a
s	h	r	e	j	o	b	f	a	l	o	m	t	e	w	i
g	e	r	u	t	m	l	u	e	e	q	e	r	e	h	t
b	l	m	c	o	a	x	m	k	a	l	r	k	v	l	u
c	p	a	t	a	k	o	e	w	s	a	i	d	l	l	c
e	t	s	o	m	e	y	o	l	e	l	t	s	i	h	w

Hands-On Activities   MY NAME: _____

Comprehension Quiz

Circle the answer that is correct.

1. Which word is not a sight word?
   a) it   **b)** cat   **c)** black

2. Which word will fit? ☐☐☐☐
   a) what   **b)** walk   **c)** ride

3. Which word finishes this sentence? *I _____ to eat apples.*
   a) when   **b)** am   **c)** like

4. Which word does not belong?
   a) toe   **b)** stop   **c)** said

5. Which sight word has two syllables?
   a) good   **b)** yellow   **c)** when

Circle **T** if the statement is TRUE **or** **F** if it is FALSE.

T   F   **a)** "Shirt" is a sight word.

T   F   **b)** "The, jump, in" are sight words.

T   F   **c)** "Crown" rhymes with brown.

T   F   **d)** "Can you give me the ball?" is a sentence made up of all sight words.

T   F   **e)** The word "know" starts with a "n" sound.

SUBTOTAL: /10

MY NAME: _____

Comprehension Quiz

1. Unscramble the words. Write the word on the line.

a) erteh _____

b) ttrpye _____

c) ckalb _____

d) aylp _____

Answer the questions in complete sentences.

2. What is a sight word? Give an example.
_____
_____
_____

3. List six sight words:
_____ _____ _____
_____ _____ _____

4. Write a sight word in each blank to finish the sentences.

a) _____ girl went to school.

b) _____ boy fell off of his bike.

c) _____ you come to my house?

d) I invited _____ of my friends to the party.

e) _____ do you live?

f) A circle is _____ .

SUBTOTAL: /19

1. that
2. what
3. new
4. black
5. saw
6. do
7. under
8. out
9. am
10. yes

Answers will vary.

---

1. with
2. good
3. must
4. soon
5. too
6. went
7. ride
8. did
9. all
10. our

Answers will vary.

---

1. look
2. make
3. funny
4. see
5. yellow
6. one
7. three
8. away
9. two

Answers will vary.

---

1. blue
2. find
3. come
4. her
5. play
6. my
7. it
8. little
9. and
10. said

Answers will vary.

---

1. can
2. I
3. run
4. not
5. to
6. for
7. help
8. is
9. we
10. jump

Answers will vary.

---

1. in
2. a
3. go
4. big
5. up
6. red
7. down
8. me
9. the
10. you

Answers will vary.

15
1. say
2. there
3. white
4. want
5. eat
6. no
7. he
8. please
9. brown
10. are

Answers will vary.

16
1. they
2. into
3. was
4. four
5. who
6. at
7. she
8. pretty
9. now
10. but

Answers will vary.

17
1. this
2. like
3. came
4. ran
5. well
6. ate
7. on
8. get
9. so
10. will

Answers will vary.

18
1. let
2. think
3. take
4. old
5. him
6. as
7. put
8. after
9. every
10. going

Answers will vary.

19
1. had
2. again
3. thank
4. walk
5. ask
6. live
7. how
8. round
9. fly
10. once

Answers will vary.

20
1. just
2. where
3. them
4. some
5. from
6. an
7. by
8. has
9. open
10. may

Answers will vary.

© CLASSROOM COMPLETE PRESS

1. any
2. know
3. stop
4. over
5. her
6. then
7. of
8. give
9. could
10. when

Answers will vary.

down	big	eat		ran	ask
jump	can	four		ride	fly
two	one	good		under	her
look	help	new		well	him
funny	three	no		yes	give
run	see	out		pretty	old

High-Frequency Sight Words CC1113

again	
know	
from	
just	
every	
thank	
them	
(33)	

	I
	a
	me
	come
	her
	up
	down
	blue
	go
	the
	play
	big
	in
	you
	(34)

EZ ✓

make	
find	
not	
my	
it	
away	
said	
(31)	

	must
	black
	saw / now
	that
	please
	did
	this
	(32)

1. Ask, after
2. Where, live
3. give, old
4. going, stop
5. Take, open
6. think
(30)

1. Do, want
2. into
3. like
4. They, pretty
5. She, there
6. He, came, ate
(29)

1. big, and
2. up, the
3. we, a, yellow
4. you, me
5. down
6. in, red
(28)

open	
over	
round	
stop	
think	
walk	
(27)	

© CLASSROOM COMPLETE PRESS

High-Frequency Sight Words CC1113

EZ ✓

1.
a) three
b) pretty
c) black
d) play

2. A sight word is a high frequency word that appears a lot in print. Sight words are words that should be known automatically. They often cannot be sounded out. (2 points for an explanation) Example: under, well, etc. (1 point for an example)

3. Any six sight words

4.
a) The
b) A
c) Can
d) all
e) Where
f) round

⋯ 49 ⋯

1. b)
2. a)
3. c)
4. a)
5. b)

a) F
b) T
c) T
d) F
e) T

⋯ 48 ⋯

Word Search Answers

⋯ 47 ⋯

Across
1. eat
3. find
5. our
6. once
7. round
9. yellow
11. who
12. red
13. thank
14. we
16. little

Down
1. every
2. too
3. four
4. down
8. under
10. white
11. when
14. want
15. know
17. two

⋯ 46 ⋯

all
ride
with
soon
good
please
went
with
want
too

⋯ 35 ⋯

over
could
walk
fly
where
open
After
take
by
old
Ask

⋯ 36 ⋯

Rhyme Time

 In the column on the left, record five sight words. Say the word. Think of other words that sound like the sight word. In the column on the right write three words that rhyme with the sight word.

Sight Word	Rhyming Words

Write the Room

Look around the classroom for sight words. Record ten of them on the lines below. Choose five and write them in sentences.

Sight Words

1. _____
2. _____
3. _____
4. _____
5. _____
6. _____
7. _____
8. _____
9. _____
10. _____

Sentences

1. _____
2. _____
3. _____
4. _____
5. _____

Take a Guess

Read each clue. Think of which sight word matches the clue. Write the word on the line in the guess column. Read the next clue and make another guess.

Clue	Guess
1. This word has _____ letters.	_____
2. This word has _____ sounds.	_____
3. This word starts with a _____.	_____
4. This word rhymes with _____.	_____
5. This word makes sense in this sentence: _____.	_____

Sight Word Tally Chart

 Choose a book from the classroom. Read the first five pages. List all of the sight words you find. Put a tally in the right column to show how many times each word appears.

Book Title: _____

Author: _____

Sight Word	Number of Times Found

Predict the Hidden Word

 Meeting Friends at the Park

On the weekend I went to the store with my mom. The store didn't

open until nine o'clock so we had a cookie first. We bought a

picnic basket, some apples, and a new bathing suit for me.

Then we went to meet our old friends at the park.

We met them by the swings and had a picnic.

After we put on our bathing suits and went for a swim.

We had a great time. I can't wait to see them again.

Endings

Write the numbers 1-5 on your paper.

1. Write the word:

2.

3. Which sight word will help you spell: _____
(_____)

4. What ending do you need to add to spell the word:
_____ ? (_____)

5. Write _____ on your paper.

Publication Listing

Ask Your Dealer About Our Complete Line

SOCIAL STUDIES - Books

ITEM #	TITLE
	DAILY LIFE SKILLS SERIES
CC5790	Daily Marketplace Skills
CC5791	Daily Social & Workplace Skills
CC5792	Daily Health & Hygiene Skills
CC5793	Daily Life Skills Big Book
	MAPPING SKILLS SERIES
CC5786	Grades PK-2 Mapping Skills with Google Earth
CC5787	Grades 3-5 Mapping Skills with Google Earth
CC5788	Grades 6-8 Mapping Skills with Google Earth
CC5789	Grades PK-8 Mapping Skills with Google Earth Big Book
	NORTH AMERICAN GOVERNMENTS SERIES
CC5757	American Government
CC5758	Canadian Government
CC5759	Mexican Government
CC5760	Governments of North America Big Book
	WORLD GOVERNMENTS SERIES
CC5761	World Political Leaders
CC5762	World Electoral Processes
CC5763	Capitalism vs. Communism
CC5777	World Politics Big Book
	WORLD CONFLICT SERIES
CC5511	American Revolutionary War
CC5500	American Civil War
CC5512	American Wars Big Book
CC5501	World War I
CC5502	World War II
CC5503	World Wars I & II Big Book
CC5505	Korean War
CC5506	Vietnam War
CC5507	Korean & Vietnam Wars Big Book
CC5508	Persian Gulf War (1990-1991)
CC5509	Iraq War (2003-2010)
CC5510	Gulf Wars Big Book
	WORLD CONTINENTS SERIES
CC5750	North America
CC5751	South America
CC5768	The Americas Big Book
CC5752	Europe
CC5753	Africa
CC5754	Asia
CC5755	Australia
CC5756	Antarctica
	WORLD CONNECTIONS SERIES
CC5782	Culture, Society & Globalization
CC5783	Economy & Globalization
CC5784	Technology & Globalization
CC5785	Globalization Big Book

VISIT: www.CLASSROOM COMPLETE PRESS.com
To view sample pages from each book

REGULAR & REMEDIAL EDUCATION
Reading Level 3-4 Grades 5-8

SOCIAL STUDIES - Software

ITEM #	TITLE
	MAPPING SKILLS SERIES
CC7770	Grades PK-2 Mapping Skills with Google Earth
CC7771	Grades 3-5 Mapping Skills with Google Earth
CC7772	Grades 6-8 Mapping Skills with Google Earth
CC7773	Grades PK-8 Mapping Skills with Google Earth Big Box

SCIENCE - Software

	SPACE AND BEYOND SERIES
CC7557	Solar System Grades 5-8
CC7558	Galaxies & the Universe Grades 5-8
CC7559	Space Travel & Technology Grades 5-8
CC7560	Space Big Box Grades 5-8
	HUMAN BODY SERIES
CC7549	Cells, Skeletal & Muscular Systems Grades 5-8
CC7550	Senses, Nervous & Respiratory Systems Grades 5-8
CC7551	Circulatory, Digestive & Reproductive Systems Grades 5-8
CC7552	Human Body Big Box Grades 5-8
	FORCE, MOTION & SIMPLE MACHINES SERIES
CC7553	Force Grades 3-8
CC7554	Motion Grades 3-8
CC7555	Simple Machines Grades 3-8
CC7556	Force, Motion & Simple Machines Big Box Grades 3-8

ENVIRONMENTAL STUDIES - Software

	CLIMATE CHANGE SERIES
CC7747	Global Warming: Causes Grades 3-8
CC7748	Global Warming: Effects Grades 3-8
CC7749	Global Warming: Reduction Grades 3-8
CC7750	Global Warming Big Box Grades 3-8

LANGUAGE ARTS - Software

CC7112	Word Families - Short Vowels Grades PK-2
CC7113	Word Families - Long Vowels Grades PK-2
CC7114	Word Families - Vowels Big Box Grades PK-2
CC7100	High Frequency Sight Words Grades PK-2
CC7101	High Frequency Picture Words Grades PK-2
CC7102	Sight & Picture Words Big Box Grades PK-2
CC7104	How to Write a Paragraph Grades 3-8
CC7105	How to Write a Book Report Grades 3-8
CC7106	How to Write an Essay Grades 3-8
CC7107	Master Writing Big Box Grades 3-8
CC7108	Reading Comprehension Grades 5-8
CC7109	Literary Devices Grades 5-8
CC7110	Critical Thinking Grades 5-8
CC7111	Master Reading Big Box Grades 5-8

SCIENCE - Books

ITEM #	TITLE
	ECOLOGY & THE ENVIRONMENT SERIES
CC4500	Ecosystems
CC4501	Classification & Adaptation
CC4502	Cells
CC4503	Ecology & The Environment Big Book
	MATTER & ENERGY SERIES
CC4504	Properties of Matter
CC4505	Atoms, Molecules & Elements
CC4506	Energy
CC4507	The Nature of Matter Big Book
	FORCE & MOTION SERIES
CC4508	Force
CC4509	Motion
CC4510	Simple Machines
CC4511	Force, Motion & Simple Machines Big Book
	SPACE & BEYOND SERIES
CC4512	Solar System
CC4513	Galaxies & The Universe
CC4514	Travel & Technology
CC4515	Space Big Book
	HUMAN BODY SERIES
CC4516	Cells, Skeletal & Muscular Systems
CC4517	Senses, Nervous & Respiratory Systems
CC4518	Circulatory, Digestive & Reproductive Systems
CC4519	Human Body Big Book

ENVIRONMENTAL STUDIES - Books

	MANAGING OUR WASTE SERIES
CC5764	Waste: At the Source
CC5765	Prevention, Recycling & Conservation
CC5766	Waste: The Global View
CC5767	Waste Management Big Book
	CLIMATE CHANGE SERIES
CC5769	Global Warming: Causes
CC5770	Global Warming: Effects
CC5771	Global Warming: Reduction
CC5772	Global Warming Big Book
	GLOBAL WATER SERIES
CC5773	Conservation: Fresh Water Resources
CC5774	Conservation: Ocean Water Resources
CC5775	Conservation: Waterway Habitat Resources
CC5776	Water Conservation Big Book
	CARBON FOOTPRINT SERIES
CC5778	Reducing Your Own Carbon Footprint
CC5779	Reducing Your School's Carbon Footprint
CC5780	Reducing Your Community's Carbon Footprint
CC5781	Carbon Footprint Big Book

LITERATURE KITS™ - Books

ITEM #	TITLE
	GRADES 1-2
CC2100	Curious George (H. A. Rey)
CC2101	Paper Bag Princess (Robert N. Munsch)
CC2102	Stone Soup (Marcia Brown)
CC2103	The Very Hungry Caterpillar (Eric Carle)
CC2104	Where the Wild Things Are (Maurice Sendak)
	GRADES 3-4
CC2300	Babe: The Gallant Pig (Dick King-Smith)
CC2301	Because of Winn-Dixie (Kate DiCamillo)
CC2302	The Tale of Despereaux (Kate DiCamillo)
CC2303	James and the Giant Peach (Roald Dahl)
CC2304	Ramona Quimby, Age 8 (Beverly Cleary)
CC2305	The Mouse and the Motorcycle (Beverly Cleary)
CC2306	Charlotte's Web (E.B. White)
CC2307	Owls in the Family (Farley Mowat)
CC2308	Sarah, Plain and Tall (Patricia MacLachlan)
CC2309	Matilda (Roald Dahl)
CC2310	Charlie & The Chocolate Factory (Roald Dahl)
CC2311	Frindle (Andrew Clements)
CC2312	M.C. Higgins, the Great (Virginia Hamilton)
CC2313	The Family Under The Bridge (N.S. Carlson)
CC2314	The Hundred Penny Box (Sharon Mathis)
CC2315	Cricket in Times Square (George Selden)
CC2316	Fantastic Mr Fox (Roald Dahl)
CC2317	The Hundred Dresses (Eleanor Estes)
CC2318	The War with Grandpa (Robert Kimmel Smith)
	GRADES 5-6
CC2500	Black Beauty (Anna Sewell)
CC2501	Bridge to Terabithia (Katherine Paterson)
CC2502	Bud, Not Buddy (Christopher Paul Curtis)
CC2503	The Egypt Game (Zilpha Keatley Snyder)
CC2504	The Great Gilly Hopkins (Katherine Paterson)
CC2505	Holes (Louis Sachar)
CC2506	Number the Stars (Lois Lowry)
CC2507	The Sign of the Beaver (E.G. Speare)
CC2508	The Whipping Boy (Sid Fleischman)
CC2509	Island of the Blue Dolphins (Scott O'Dell)
CC2510	Underground to Canada (Barbara Smucker)
CC2511	Loser (Jerry Spinelli)
CC2512	The Higher Power of Lucky (Susan Patron)
CC2513	Kira-Kira (Cynthia Kadohata)
CC2514	Dear Mr. Henshaw (Beverly Cleary)
CC2515	The Summer of the Swans (Betsy Byars)
CC2516	Shiloh (Phyllis Reynolds Naylor)
CC2517	A Single Shard (Linda Sue Park)
CC2518	Hoot (Carl Hiaasen)
CC2519	Hatchet (Gary Paulsen)
CC2520	The Giver (Lois Lowry)
CC2521	The Graveyard Book (Neil Gaiman)
CC2522	The View From Saturday (E.L. Konigsburg)
CC2523	Hattie Big Sky (Kirby Larson)
CC2524	When You Reach Me (Rebecca Stead)
CC2525	Criss Cross (Lynne Rae Perkins)
CC2526	A Year Down Yonder (Richard Peck)
CC2527	Maniac Magee (Jerry Spinelli)

LITERATURE KITS™ - Books

ITEM #	TITLE
CC2528	From the Mixed-Up Files of Mrs. Basil E. Frankweiler (E.L. Konigsburg)
CC2529	Sing Down the Moon (Scott O'Dell)
CC2530	The Phantom Tollbooth (Norton Juster)
CC2531	Gregor the Overlander (Suzanne Collins)
	GRADES 7-8
CC2700	Cheaper by the Dozen (Frank B. Gilbreth)
CC2701	The Miracle Worker (William Gibson)
CC2702	The Red Pony (John Steinbeck)
CC2703	Treasure Island (Robert Louis Stevenson)
CC2704	Romeo & Juliet (William Shakespeare)
CC2705	Crispin: The Cross of Lead (Avi)
CC2706	Call It Courage (Armstrong Sperry)
CC2707	The Boy in the Striped Pajamas (John Boyne)
CC2708	The Westing Game (Ellen Raskin)
CC2709	The Cay (Theodore Taylor)
CC2710	The Hunger Games (Suzanne Collins)
	GRADES 9-12
CC2001	To Kill A Mockingbird (Harper Lee)
CC2002	Angela's Ashes (Frank McCourt)
CC2003	The Grapes of Wrath (John Steinbeck)
CC2004	The Good Earth (Pearl S. Buck)
CC2005	The Road (Cormac McCarthy)
CC2006	The Old Man and the Sea (Ernest Hemingway)
CC2007	Lord of the Flies (William Golding)
CC2008	The Color Purple (Alice Walker)
CC2009	The Outsiders (S.E. Hinton)
CC2010	Hamlet (William Shakespeare)
CC2011	The Great Gatsby (F. Scott Fitzgerald)
CC2012	The Adventures of Huckleberry Finn (Mark Twain)
CC2013	Macbeth (William Shakespeare)
CC2014	Fahrenheit 451 (Ray Bradbury)

LANGUAGE ARTS - Books

ITEM #	TITLE
CC1110	Word Families - Short Vowels Grades K-1
CC1111	Word Families - Long Vowels Grades K-1
CC1112	Word Families - Vowels Big Book Grades K-1
CC1113	High Frequency Sight Words Grades K-1
CC1114	High Frequency Picture Words Grades K-1
CC1115	Sight & Picture Words Big Book Grades K-1
CC1100	How to Write a Paragraph Grades 5-8
CC1101	How to Write a Book Report Grades 5-8
CC1102	How to Write an Essay Grades 5-8
CC1103	Master Writing Big Book Grades 5-8
CC1116	Reading Comprehension Grades 5-8
CC1117	Literary Devices Grades 5-8
CC1118	Critical Thinking Grades 5-8
CC1119	Master Reading Big Book Grades 5-8
CC1106	Reading Response Forms: Grades 1-2
CC1107	Reading Response Forms: Grades 3-4
CC1108	Reading Response Forms: Grades 5-6
CC1109	Reading Response Forms Big Book: Grades 1-6

MATHEMATICS - Software

ITEM #	TITLE
	PRINCIPLES & STANDARDS OF MATH SERIES
CC7315	Grades PK-2 Five Strands of Math Big Box
CC7316	Grades 3-5 Five Strands of Math Big Box
CC7317	Grades 6-8 Five Strands of Math Big Box

MATHEMATICS - Books

ITEM #	TITLE
	TASK SHEETS
CC3100	Grades PK-2 Number & Operations Task Sheets
CC3101	Grades PK-2 Algebra Task Sheets
CC3102	Grades PK-2 Geometry Task Sheets
CC3103	Grades PK-2 Measurement Task Sheets
CC3104	Grades PK-2 Data Analysis & Probability Task Sheets
CC3105	Grades PK-2 Five Strands of Math Big Book Task Sheets
CC3106	Grades 3-5 Number & Operations Task Sheets
CC3107	Grades 3-5 Algebra Task Sheets
CC3108	Grades 3-5 Geometry Task Sheets
CC3109	Grades 3-5 Measurement Task Sheets
CC3110	Grades 3-5 Data Analysis & Probability Task Sheets
CC3111	Grades 3-5 Five Strands of Math Big Book Task Sheets
CC3112	Grades 6-8 Number & Operations Task Sheets
CC3113	Grades 6-8 Algebra Task Sheets
CC3114	Grades 6-8 Geometry Task Sheets
CC3115	Grades 6-8 Measurement Task Sheets
CC3116	Grades 6-8 Data Analysis & Probability Task Sheets
CC3117	Grades 6-8 Five Strands of Math Big Book Task Sheets
	DRILL SHEETS
CC3200	Grades PK-2 Number & Operations Drill Sheets
CC3201	Grades PK-2 Algebra Drill Sheets
CC3202	Grades PK-2 Geometry Drill Sheets
CC3203	Grades PK-2 Measurement Drill Sheets
CC3204	Grades PK-2 Data Analysis & Probability Drill Sheets
CC3205	Grades PK-2 Five Strands of Math Big Book Drill Sheets
CC3206	Grades 3-5 Number & Operations Drill Sheets
CC3207	Grades 3-5 Algebra Drill Sheets
CC3208	Grades 3-5 Geometry Drill Sheets
CC3209	Grades 3-5 Measurement Drill Sheets
CC3210	Grades 3-5 Data Analysis & Probability Drill Sheets
CC3211	Grades 3-5 Five Strands of Math Big Book Drill Sheets
CC3212	Grades 6-8 Number & Operations Drill Sheets
CC3213	Grades 6-8 Algebra Drill Sheets
CC3214	Grades 6-8 Geometry Drill Sheets
CC3215	Grades 6-8 Measurement Drill Sheets
CC3216	Grades 6-8 Data Analysis & Probability Drill Sheets
CC3217	Grades 6-8 Five Strands of Math Big Book Drill Sheets
	TASK & DRILL SHEETS
CC3300	Grades PK-2 Number & Operations Task & Drill Sheets
CC3301	Grades PK-2 Algebra Task & Drill Sheets
CC3302	Grades PK-2 Geometry Task & Drill Sheets
CC3303	Grades PK-2 Measurement Task & Drill Sheets
CC3304	Grades PK-2 Data Analysis & Probability Task & Drills
CC3306	Grades 3-5 Number & Operations Task & Drill Sheets
CC3307	Grades 3-5 Algebra Task & Drill Sheets
CC3308	Grades 3-5 Geometry Task & Drill Sheets
CC3309	Grades 3-5 Measurement Task & Drill Sheets
CC3310	Grades 3-5 Data Analysis & Probability Task & Drills
CC3312	Grades 6-8 Number & Operations Task & Drill Sheets
CC3313	Grades 6-8 Algebra Task & Drill Sheets
CC3314	Grades 6-8 Geometry Task & Drill Sheets
CC3315	Grades 6-8 Measurement Task & Drill Sheets
CC3316	Grades 6-8 Data Analysis & Probability Task & Drills

www.CLASSROOMCOMPLETEPRESS.com